Job Hunting:

THE INSIDER'S GUIDE TO JOB HUNTING AND CAREER CHANGE: LEARN HOW TO BEAT THE JOB MARKET

Emily Anderson

© 2017

COPYRIGHT

Job Hunting: The Insider's Guide to Job Hunting and Career Change: Learn How to Beat the Job Market

By Emily Anderson

TABLE OF CONTENTS

CHAPTER 1. SO YOU'RE LOOKING FOR A JOB...

"If it's your job to eat a frog, it's best to do it first thing in the morning. And if it's your job to eat two frogs, it's best to eat the biggest one first." - Mark Twain

Looking for a job is notoriously one of the most stressful things in life. There are many steps in the process, and each step is another risk of failure or rejection. Until you land what you are - or are not - looking for, hunting for a job can feel like overwhelming.

The trick is to remain levelheaded at approaching the steps one by one. This book is aimed at helping you do just that. We will take you step-by-step through the process with examples, worksheets, brainstorming sessions, and more.

BEGINNING YOUR JOB HUNT

It is called a job hunt for good reason; it is literally a hunt. You need to know how big your prey is and come prepared with what you need to take it down. This preparation begins earlier than you may expect.

Before you begin crafting your resume, drafting your cover letter, or even scrolling through job boards for hours on end, you must know exactly which jungle you are looking to forage. If you are already in the career you wish to progress in, then congratulations! You have already done most of the legwork for job hunting. You know the lingo, you have seen other people do it, you have connections and you have knowledge. However, if you are looking to move to another city, it can change the way the prey is approached.

If you are just starting out, or are an industry-changer, you will have to take it from the top.

It is important to know the industry you are in, or looking to get into; you have to walk the walk and talk the talk. This is for many reasons. Everything from how you dress to how you speak can vary depending on where you are looking to work.

Most people have heard the expression: Dress for the job you want, not the job you have. There is a lot of power in going to work looking to achieve more, do more, and be more. It resonates. That is often why people wear suits to interviews (even if it may not be necessary – but more on that later).

For instance, an astronaut would not show up to an interview at an auto body repair shop talking about their knowledge of astrophysics. That is not what is going to be of use in the job to come. Instead, they could boast their knowledge of mathematics and engineering, as it would relate to the tasks at hand.

In terms that are a bit more down to earth, let us say this: a car salesman who is looking to become an insurance broker would have a lot of *transferrable skills*, like negotiation, working with a book of business, client-relations, etc., but there are things about the industry they inherently would not know. The task at hand would be to learn some of the career jargon. They should never have to ask what something in a job description means or be surprised by an unfamiliar term in an interview.

It is important to study up on the buzzwords. Be warned! A lot of the time they includes several acronyms.

TIP: Don't shoot yourself in the foot by reciting an acronym letter by letter. A lot of the time they are supposed to be read and understood as a word. I: software-as-a-service, or SAAS, should be spoken out as "Sass" within the industry. It's important to sound like you know what you are talking about so it doesn't sound like you'll need a lot of training. When you're looking to get hired, it's your job to do all the work on the back end without having to resort to learning or asking on the fly.

Aside from talking the talk, walk the walk. Know who the top competitors are and what sets your target-employer apart. It will be these little details of knowing the industry that will set you apart and launch you ahead.

If you've been in the industry that you're applying to already, this will be secondhand.

TIP: Twitter can be a great tool for getting daily doses of industry updates, and most everyone who's anyone has a handle. Find a list of companies, CEOs, and influencers to follow. A little light scrolling every day will help you get the latest news and get you more comfortable amongst a group of industry professionals.

Twitter scrolling or reading through newsletters is just to fill your spare time. It is important not to get overly excited about what other people are doing. Do some reflecting, and realize, honestly, what your strengths and weaknesses are and which jobs that you are best fit for. If there was something in your last job that you hated, try to move away from that in your next job, or, better yet, grow from it.

Knowing all of this will help you better understand how to target possible employers.

Even if there is no open job posted, you can put yourself on an employer's radar through social media. Follow the threads that they do, and do not be afraid to engage in commentary [so long as it's relevant and thoughtful]. These moments will prove that you are very engaged in the industry and can provide valuable insights or feedback in relation to the work you either have or seek. They can also get you a chance to chat with someone before a job is posted!

KNOWING HOW TO NETWORK

ONLINE

Creating an online presence is vital to knowing how to network. By, literally, social networking, you are opening the opportunity for conversation that most people have a hard time doing face-to-face (more on that shortly.)

Though social networks are often used primarily for personal use, there still exists opportunity to get in touch with people within your target industry. It's a great way to showcase yourself in alignment with your interests.

Social media also provides a great way to maintain your network without getting too personal. LinkedIn is a preferred way for many professions to keep in touch with old colleagues. By remaining in the same network, you keep that bridge in good standing. They are still accessible to you should you want to share ideas. Best-case scenario, they work for an employer that interests you. So long as they are in good standing there, it is a great person to open the door for you.

EXAMPLE:

Hey Melissa!

How are things going at Dorchester and Dorchester? I have been considering exploring some of my options at other companies and was hoping I could pick your brain a bit to see if I could see myself there and if it's worth applying. Would you be available to meet for coffee sometime next week? I would be happy to come by your part of town if that works for you. Let me know!

As long as you are asking for insight and not looking for handouts, meeting for coffee is a great networking strategy. Social media has become a great Rolodex for allowing those meetings to happen.

Following on other sites like Twitter, if you are comfortable enough to do so, can also be a good way to remain in the contact with colleagues. Many times, people in your field will have similar interests, professionally or publicly at least, to speak about those things. That could create opportunity for you to get a first-hand referral to job networking, posting, or events from others within the industry. If you are looking to break into an industry and know people within it, it can be helpful to follow them for the same reason. If they have a notably professional profile, it can come in handy.

It could even break the ice at a meet up. Referencing a commonly known source of information on social media and how it has influenced or impacted your job is a good skill to learn. Twitter has become one of the most commonly recognized and regarded outlets for a company or individual to make a statement. It can be a great way to bridge the gap between social media and social networking.

Networking is key to job-searching and even just job fulfillment. Expanding your *network,* or those you have contact with in your professional life, offers opportunities for getting yourself on career paths you may not have otherwise.

CHAPTER 2. YOUR RESUME

"Costumes are the first impression that you have of the character before they open their mouth - it really does establish who they are." - Colleen Atwood

Unless you have a pre-existing relationship, your resume is the first thing an employer sees when you apply for a job. This is your chance at a first impression. Your resume must present, in whole, exactly who you are as a professional.

WHAT TO INCLUDE IN YOUR CV

The perfect resume, as you may have guessed, varies from industry to industry. Most resumes need a lot of the same information, which we will be discussing in depth here.

The objective is normally the first stop on a resume, when writing it and, in turn, reading it. "Most objectives state things as generic as 'I am seeking a role to further my career in the hospitality industry that will help me grown in the field.' That is already assumed and obvious since you are applying to the position," says Laura Attewell, Human Resources Professional based in Chicago, Illinois.

1. Updated contact information

The easiest part of completing a resume is including how to reach you. That does not mean it deserves any less attention

"You would be surprised how many qualified candidates are unreachable due to incorrect phone numbers or misspelled email addresses," says Laura. Make sure you check, double check, and triple check your info is correct before sending your resume anywhere.

Another helpful hint from Laura, is to ensure your resume city and state reflect the position's location.

"If you are relocating to another state and already applying to jobs there, the recruiter won't always know that," she says. "Most positions are only looking for local candidates; update your resume address accordingly to get your foot in the door with an interview so you can explain your situation."

TIP: Your Street and mailing address are unnecessary on a resume; city and state will suffice.

2. Always list your current or most recent job first

It is nearly always assumed that your most relevant experience is the most recent. You'll want to have a very neat list of where you are now and how you got to there.

Begin with your title and at what company you hold it. Then list your start month through "present" or the end date.

DO include both month and year, not just year. Both are necessary.

DON'T put specific dates. Too many numbers or dates on a resume become distracting from the meat of the resume.

Example: Head of Customer Relations, January 2015 - August 2017

3. Resume vs. Memoir

When listing your accomplishments or duties, keep it digestible. This is one place in life where you are not necessarily confined to complete sentences. Feel free to list your accomplishments a little more than you would elaborate on them.

BAD:

Customer Success Manager, Tech Inc.

September 23, 2013 - present

- At my current job, I work with our biggest partners ensuring that they are getting what they need from our technology

GOOD:

Customer Success Manager, Technology. Inc.

September 2013 - present

- Manage the day-to-day customer relationship for partnerships and large brands

- Align Client Search and Content Marketing objectives with the value and functionality of our technology

DON'T turn your resume into a letter. You can explain some of your accomplishments in full in your cover letter or, better yet, in the interview

The resume should be how you highlight your accomplishments to attract an employer so that

they request an interview. The interview is where you'll be asked to elaborate more; save it for then.

Ideally, if you are starting out or a mid-level professional, your resume should fit onto **one page***.

According to Time magazine and agreed upon by many industry professionals, recruiters or hiring managers, on average, scan a resume for 6 seconds before they make a decision. They normally have hundreds of resumes to scan through daily. That is a brief window of time to make you stand out among the crowd.

Remember those keywords in an industry that we mentioned in Chapter 1? They are incredibly vital to making your resume stand out. The ability to speak the lingo of your field will make you sound like the expert professional they want. Ensure you are using them properly and that they flow with the rest of the information presented.

Your resume should reflect your relevant work experience as it pertains to the job to which you are applying. Keep it confined to your professional experience. It is not necessary to list jobs you held prior to breaking into your field unless you are a newcomer.

As a benchmark, if you have been in your industry for less than five years, leave out anything that is not relevant. You will not need to include any part-time work unless it helps to depict your transition.

If there is a *gap* in your resume, or a period of time during which you were not working, it is okay to have that included, but be ready to explain. It will most likely be asked about. Include any side project you had to make up for this period of time. Side projects can be included on the bottom of your resume. If it is a tangible project that can be accessed like a blog or an e-book, write the dates worked on and include either a link or a title of how it can be accessed.

If you took a sabbatical, list that as well. If you traveled the world for 3 months, list that. It does make you sound well rounded. There are many reasons why someone might have left work for a period of time. The only thing that makes it fishy is if you try to hide it.

Sometimes there are other extenuating circumstances that prevented you from working. In this case, an objective is a useful section to include at the top of your resume. You will be able to write in your reason for the time of missing work.

In essence, you do not want any time not working to seem like time off. Make sure that you account for the time with substantial accomplishments, such as volunteer work or family matters.

After you have finished highlighting your work experience, you can highlight add any additions that you feel necessary, such as clubs, awards attained (that are relevant to the work you are applying to do), or other achievements. It is also important to list your skills. If your job is one that requires familiarity or fluency in a program, list that on your resume. Listing applications you work with will help you appear in more searches, as well as bring a sense of relief to an interviewer – one less thing that needs to be trained!

5. Spell check

There is often little to no leeway for grammar or spelling mistakes. If employers are going to take the time to speak with you, they're going to want to ensure you took the time on your end to have a clean resume. You are, after all, applying to a job. They will not be impressed with, nor want to give a job to, someone who does a sloppy job on their resume.

"This is the personal preference, but I will throw out applications for hourly employees if it has 3 or more errors and salaried manager applications if there is one error," Laura Attewell details.

Don't get thrown out. Also, don't only rely on spell check. Have someone else look over your resume before you send it out. Another pair of eyes may catch an error the computer has not.

6. Tangibles

Especially if you are in a sales role numbers will count for everything in gauging your candidacy. Be specific when you speak of targets hit. It will be a better way to illustrate your success to your potential employer.

Example:

Exceeded quota by 104% in Q3

Achieved 100% retention rate for new clients signed in 2016

It is much more impressive to see that you had a goal to meet and exceeded it than just saying that you did your duty.

7. Languages

Listing your ability to speak another language is also going to be a major factor in candidacy. It gives you an edge of being able to communicate with a wider audience and makes you appearworldlier. Bonus points if your interviewer can speak the same language.

After you have assembled all the proper experience highlights on your resume, if there is room, take the opportunity to highlight yourself. Include a brief line about your interests outside of work. Remember that if you get past the robot, your resume will be in front of a human. Try to find something to relate about.

Example:

Interests: rock-climbing, Dan Brown novels, craft coffee, collecting 80s funk records

Try things that stand out and show you have a deep interest in something.

USING A RESUME TEMPLATE

There are a lot of very clean, helpful templates you can find online or on your computer. Google Docs has a very helpful, very clean resume for a good start.

For these templates, be careful. This goes along with double-checking. Ensure that you don't fall into the mistake of submitting a resume that still says "PUT PREVIOUS WORK EXPERIENCE HERE." Take it out! It shouldn't look at all like a template when you are done customizing it.

Checklist for your resume:

- Spell check!

- Updated contact information including city and state of job

- Accurate dates of employment

- Proper verb tenses for each role

- Numbers, if necessary, depicting your successes

- Some interests you hold, if space permits

- Languages you speak, if applicable

* There are exceptions to the "one-page rule." If you have been in your field for more than 10 years, it is expected that you have a little bit more to present. Academic, engineering, medical, or technical fields may exceed one page to accommodate your experience and accomplishments. Just ensure that your most important roles and accomplishments are not concealed.

THE EVER-EVOLVING ART OF THE

COVER LETTER

As job searching shifts and changes to accommodate the way we use technology, so does how we apply to jobs. Historically speaking, it was necessary to submit your resume attached with a cover letter (attached on top, by either staple or otherwise as the literal cover to your application) expressing why you are interested in the job.

Since the days of submitting a paper resume are becoming antiquated, so is the traditional sense of the cover. More and more companies are foregoing the cover letter in replace of online applications that have questions to be answered before it can be submitted.

The cover letter is not completely dead yet. It is still important to understand when one is necessary and how to construct something that will get your message across, display your worth, and not bore the hiring manager.

Like your resume, the updated cover letter should still include your contact information. It is not always going to be the case that these files are sent together, or looked at simultaneously. Make sure you have your contact information listed and that it matches what is on your resume.

The body of cover letters has not changed in terms of what employers are looking for. They want to know who you are and why you are interested and qualified in this job. Traditionally, this would be done in several paragraphs.

Example:

To Whom It May Concern,

I am currently a Customer Service Representative YG Global where I conduct tours and sell office space for the center. I serve as the primary backup for the General Manager as well as trainer and mentor for new employees. I am the first point of contact for customers regarding accounts receivable and follow the collections process by initiating verbal communication with clients. I tend to questions concerning invoices and resolve disputes. I update office pricing and monitor future availability.

I have a strong interest in business, sales and advertising. I want to learn more about the media planning process and would love a position as Pricing and Planning Analyst.

I have a strong work ethic and I am an excellent communicator. I have experience with Microsoft Word, Excel, Power Point, Outlook, Final Cut Pro and Photoshop.

What is wrong with this cover letter starts with the first line: To Whom It May Concern. Unless you are completely unable to uncover whom you might be addressing, do not put this. It has become so insincere and sets very few letters apart from another.

Instead, try to find the name of the hiring manager you will be submitting to. This is often an easily accessible piece of information on LinkedIn.

If a name is inaccessible, use something a little less formal such as "Dear Hiring Manager."

The second issue with this cover letter is that it spends too much time talking specifically about things that could be (and should be) found on the resume. You have very limited resources to make an impact on an employer. Choose wisely in how you use your words. The cover letter is a place where you should be able to flex your personality a little bit more freely.

What makes this a good cover letter is that is lists intangible qualities (a list of good intangible qualities will follow later in this book.) These are things that might not be strikingly apparent on a resume, but may be seen a little more through different practices.

Though it could have been elaborated on a little bit more, it is the closest the letter comes to having some originally and pizzazz.

A better cover letter would look like this:

Dear Hiring Manager,

I'm excited to be writing you this letter in regards to your job posting for a role in your advertising department. I have spent the last two years' since my graduation interning with live shows, learning the ins and outs of the entertainment industry. Through all of the changing landscapes of television, one thing remains the same: advertisers need a platform on which to be heard.

This fact became apparent to me and sparked my interest in engaging with the media team on organizing ad space for our weekly shows. I have been given the opportunity to work closely with this team, but it is my hope that I will be able to work on an advertising team.

That is why I'm interested in your open position. My preparation has come in the steady workflow I have had over the years, and I am confident in my adaptability in learning the details of a new role.

This letter gives a little bit more insight into a candidate and their interests and motivations. It also sheds more of a spotlight on the experience, rather than rehashing in sentence forms all of the things that are on the resume.

If you have successfully created an image for yourself via the cover letter, be sure to end with the best way to contact you.

Pout the ball in their court and create an enticing profile for the hiring manager.

LinkedIn

Social media is one of the biggest influences on job searching. It has been ringing through the air since Facebook exploded into common practice to ensure that it is spic and span; you are a quick Google search away from getting a bad reputation from a potential employer.

Assuming you have kept a clean (or at least privatized) social media presence, it is also important to keep tabs on your LinkedIn page.

LinkedIn is the new resume. It is the easiest, most accessible means for employers to see who you are as a professional. It is more than just a resume; it can act as a portfolio, as well be a place to file your references (in the form of endorsements). Here is where you can collect all of the information about your job history and duties, your connections to the industry, what you are involved in, what projects you completed, and what people have to say about you in a professional capacity. Each one of these things will become vital creating a strong profile - one employers will be attracted to.

LinkedIn is where a majority of recruiters and hiring manager begin their search. **If you are applying online, make sure that your resume matches your LinkedIn profile.** They will often look at both.

As mentioned before, keywords are pertinent to being landed on. The recruiting process often begins with a search for companies in the industry wherein the employees are equipped the skills being sought. If they don't target companies, they will target duties.

Many recruiters use what is called the "Boolean Search." This method is a way of stringing together keywords, from most important to secondary and so on, in order to find people who may include them in their profile.

Example: A recruiter looking for a HR professional may write in a Boolean search "Human Resources AND policy AND employee relations"

Another thing to look out for when you expect to be a hit in a search is what NOT to have. Boolean Searches can be formulated in a way that they can exclude profiles with certain aspects.

Example: "human resources NOT recruiter"

The pitfalls of the Boolean search are that it can be exclusive, even when it is not meant to be. In terms of the above HR search, one may have included in the explanation that they had "implemented policies" on their LinkedIn but not the specific, singular format of explaining a situation in which they implemented a new policy (singular).

The more thorough your profile is in explanation, the better your chances of getting landed on.

Another difference between your resume and your LinkedIn profile is that once your profile is discovered, so is your face. Make sure your profile picture stands out in a way that is professional and appropriate for your field.

Someone applying to for a job conducting market research for a pharmaceutical company will not have the same profile picture as someone applying to be a stage costume designer.

Tips for the perfect profile picture:

- Don't have a busy background. Make it plain, ideally white or black, so that you are the main focus of the photo.

- Crop it! You rarely need a full body shot. The ideal photo begins at your shoulders.

- Clarity! Make sure you're recognizable and, more importantly, up to date. If you have blonde hair but it's black in your profile picture, it's already outdated.

HOW TO BUILD A STRONG LINKEDIN

PROFILE

Just as you check your Twitter or Facebook, you should check your LinkedIn. Checking back often helps you to stay up to speed on what many other professionals in your industry are talking about or getting involved with.

The same goes for you. When people see your profile, they should know everything on your resume and more. This is a great chance to include a link to a marketing campaign you worked on, an article you wrote, or even an event you attended. Just make sure it is included in the proper section. If an employer is intrigued by your resume or job experience, they will have the opportunity to dive deeper into your accomplishments.

Producer
Major League Baseball
Mar 2014 – Nov 2016 • 2 yrs 9 mos

Media (1)

Full Count Team Teases

Listing a side project on your resume will help lead them to the right place. If you have a link listed or a project listed on your LinkedIn or resume, it could be the extra facet that sets you apart from another candidate.

The proper place for these projects is within the field of your position. The beauty of LinkedIn is that it is a clear-cut map to one's career. It makes most sense to augment a listing as a "photojournalist" with photos you have taken within that field, just as you would put a video you produced under the title of "Production Assistant."

Even when you are still at a job, you can start looking for your next. LinkedIn makes it easy to job-hunt without unveiling yourself to your current employer. There is an option that allows you to be visible to other companies as "open to opportunities" that will automatically block any internal employees from being aware you are searching.

The ball is also in your court to build your online network.

Networking is a huge part of the LinkedIn experience. Being connected to like-minded professionals could be the catalyst for your career. Like scrolling the Twitter feed, a well-tailored

LinkedIn feed will always have someone talking about what you want to hear.

Joining groups is a great way to connect with professionals. There are many different types of groups you can join to make more connections, from heritage-focused groups to industry-centric. Find some that speak to you and ask to join! Bear in mind that whichever groups you choose to join will be visible to employers or potential employers (or your current!). Choose wisely.

LinkedIn also offers the opportunity to follow companies you are specifically interested in. If you follow a company, you will get the updates they post in addition to the jobs that open. It could be a useful tool for someone looking to get into a specific company.

There could be opportunities to network there, too! Try connecting with some professionals who work for your ideal employer.

If you are sending messages to people within the company, be careful not to blind them with a connection request that is unexpected. Always send a message to explain your position, or just request to network.

Check out their profile. What are some striking similarities?

Example:

Hi Brian,

I see you graduated from Texas State the year before I did. I'd love to connect in hopes that we may be able to network more about the film industry.

Something like that! Make everything you do personalized. Everyone, even in the business of business, wants to feel like they are being noticed.

CREATING YOUR PORTFOLIO

Imagine you are in the seat of power as the hiring manager. There are two resumes in front of you - one that details a long work experience creating projects for several clients over a long period of time, the other a short resume supplemented by a detailed portfolio.

Even if the hiring manager is impressed by a long, fulfilled work history, it is going to be the work that is set right before their eyes that makes the biggest impact. It is human nature! To have tangible work presented before you even get to meet face to face will do half of the work for you. It will cut out the time that would have otherwise been spent with a back-and-forth dialogue about a request for samples or projects complete. It nurtures another very intrinsic human nature of wanting to get the most from someone with the least amount of energy expended.

For professionals in the creative field, a portfolio holds just as much weight (if not more) in your hiring potential. There are many types of jobs that have a creative aspect. From painters and photographers to detectives and chefs, there are many ways to supplement your resume through your portfolio.

1. Have variety

When you are displaying your work, you are sometimes prone to choose your favorite pieces. Keep in mind people's' tastes are different. There are variables regarding your work that may translate better than others. Maybe you're used to photographing still life, but your employer has a keen interest for profiles. Make sure not to limit yourself to your own preferences or specialty.

If you are applying to be a mural-painter for the parks in the city, you will undoubtedly choose to provide paintings you have completed. Your paintings will be your chance to reflect what they are looking for and show that you are able to provide the service and complete the task. You do not want to limit yourself here. There will still be use for variants, such as your drawings. Having variety proves to your employer that you are not limited to one specific thing. Especially in artistic fields, it will go a long way in getting jobs to know that you have the eye and the skill to stretch your talent. Include artwork you have drawn with various media, such as charcoal or pencil. Having this variety will prove to your employer that you have many skills to go about your tasks.

2. Curate the highlights

This almost goes without saying (but must be said anyway); display only your best work. Deciding what that is could be the tricky part. Ask for help. Talk to some of your peers, mentors, friends and family. Have them look at your work or reflect on what they have seen you produce. What stood out the most to them? What struck them? It will not always be your favorite project that will resonate the most with the hiring manager

Think of it this way: perhaps you completed a painted portrait of your cat. It could be a tricky task, as your cat most likely will not want to sit still for you to capture the details necessary in a still instant. You will have to take a lot of time to get the brush-strokes just right, get the detailing spot on, and capture the demeanor of your cat. You know your cat best.

When it is all said and done, to you, you have created a masterpiece.

The problem is - your employer does not know your cat. Though the picture may seem perfect to you, those exact strokes completed may fall flat on someone who has not met your cat or, worse, does not like cats.

A better option for your portfolio may include a painting you have done of a famous monument in your city. Catching the perfect light of the sunset beyond a bridge is a skill and a project that speaks to a wider variety of people. Try to choose from your artwork that is going to stand out for the right reasons.

Side note: If that standout piece is your cat, include it! Just be sure that it will wow your audience.

Creating a portfolio is not exclusive to the visual arts. In some ways, you can make a portfolio for anyone who wants to see it. A chef can make a portfolio of recipes they have created. A hairstylist can make a portfolio of clients and haircuts. There are many opportunities in which you can showcase your talents.

Be sure that it is appreciated and truly a powerful tool if you are going to share it with a potential employer.

3. Supplementary resources

The portfolio should not just be a photo-book, but also a museum. Elaborate on your work through memos, press releases, or performance reviews. These types of credentials will be a way for your work to seem relevant. You are not just trying to get past the gatekeeper; you are hoping to be a successful employee. The best way to be given the chance is to prove that you have been a successful employee in the past.

If you are just starting out in your field, include some of your best-graded projects in school, as well as some of your personal projects. Do not stifle yourself with only things people have recognized. Have the confidence and conviction to present the full breadth of your abilities.

CHAPTER 3. WORKING WITH

RECUITERS

When you feel overwhelmed just by reading Chapters 1 and 2 by all of your hard work doing some introspective reflecting, it might be time to get some fresh eyes on what you have compiled. A recruiter can be the best, unbiased source of letting you know how things will look to potential employers. It is their job to be your coach in the process of preparing you, and your advocate in presenting and representing you to employers.

However, there can be some instances when the recruiter's best interest is not yours.

A GOOD RECRUITER: will give you several options and work with you to find the best one for you.

A BAD RECRUITER: will throw you in front of several opportunities, hoping one sticks and the transaction is a quick one.

A good recruiter should not stress you out more than the job - they should be the ones who help you sort through options.

WHAT TO LOOK FOR IN A GOOD

RECRUITER

Before we get into the good and bad, there is another very important difference in recruiters: **internal and external**. Some other common names they may refer to themselves as are *in-house or agency* recruiters. Let's talk more about how to tell the difference; it is an important one.

In-house, or internal, recruiters work for the company that is doing the hiring. It is important for you to remember that internal recruiters work for the company that you hope to work for. When dealing with an internal recruiter, be sure to present your best self. You want to be a person they can envision as a co-worker. They also want to you to be someone that their boss will approve of. In a way, they are responsible for the future of their entire company. You will want to make a very good impression.

WHY THIS MATTERS

The internal recruiter is the gatekeeper, also known as the HR department. Often, they get the first call but not the last time. For you to get to the rest of the interviewers, you must first get the approval of the internal recruiter. This means you have a little work to do.

Before you talk to the recruiter, you have to understand the company you are applying to. **You should never go into an interview call and ask questions that you could have researched on your own.** The purpose of the call is to boost your resume and make you seem worth meeting with more members of the team.

Normally, it is NOT the internal recruiter who will make the final decision. You will have to meet with other members of the team and leaders to make your impression again. Make sure you do your research on them as well. Find them on LinkedIn and make sure you know their role. It won't be overbearing to them if you know a little bit about them like their last company or where they went to school. It will show that you were proactive.

PROS: Working with an internal recruiter already allows you access to the company you are applying to. This expedites the process for you; you are already knocking directly at their door. Make sure you are someone they want to let in!

CONS: You must tiptoe a little bit more with internal recruiters. If you are working with them it is assumed you are already interested in this company. There is a lot less room for questions about industry competitors.

Internal recruiters are not there to help you revise your resume or discuss career opportunities. They are specifically the ones who have the hiring power for a role you've chosen to apply to. Choose wisely.

External recruiters often work for a staffing or talent agency. These types of agencies are connected to several companies and are tasked with connecting job seekers with the hirers. When working with these recruiters, you are a little bit freer to explain what you are looking for. They are responsible for helping you be matched a job that is best for you.

Communication is key if you are working with a recruiter on your job search. They should be involved from beginning to end in hunting for the role you want. As opposed to internal recruiters, you have much more liberty to ask external recruiters questions about the industry and the companies they work with. They should be able to answer a lot of questions pertaining to reputation, leaders, and job fulfillment.

Another thing they are the experts in is dealing with several types of clients. They will have placed candidates in companies before, so they know some things to look out for in terms of

Some questions for external recruiters:

How long have you been recruiting?

How many people have you placed in similar roles to mine?

If they have a job ready to present to you off the bat, there are a few other questions you need to gauge before taking the plunge, such as:

- For how long has this job been open?
- How long is the interview process?
- What types of qualifications of mine stood out as a good fit for this role?

These questions will help you better understand the role and where the recruiter is coming from. If they are being honest in wanting to find you the best role for your skillset, these answers will make you confident in your decision to work with them. Be wary of any recruiter that does not want to answer your questions. It should be a give and take.

What External Recruiters Should Assist With:

1. Resume help

Assuming you are a good fit for the role the recruiter put in front of you, your resume will be the first stop in preparing you for the process of being submitted. Resume help could go from constructing a resume from ground up or completely redesigning an existing one. The recruiter will know what it should look like at a glance and what information is going to be the deciding factor for hiring managers.

Since we know that your resume may get as little as six seconds to be reviewed, those six seconds have to be impressive and enticing enough to read further. Make sure the recruiter takes more time on your resume.

TIP: Ask about buzzwords*! There is always a new technology out or a new style coming into popularity. Your recruiter should be able to tell you what that is and how to implement it into your resume. That is what the hiring manager will be looking for before they skip your resume.

*see chapter 8 for your guide to understanding technology buzzwords

Having the recruiter's eyes on your resume will also be a good way to make sure you know it looks good. They are the people who are expected to be career professionals. They will also be representing you through the process of interviewing. They should make it their goal to have as much pride in your background as you have.

2. Options

A good recruiter will be an expert on the industry they are trying to get you a job in. As an expert, they will have first-hand experience dealing with like-minded professionals.

An expert will also know exactly what the job entails as well as several other intangibles of a job-search. By knowing the industry, they'll know those in it and where they work. It's the simple nature of communication.

*see chapter 8 for your guide to understanding technology buzzwords

Having the recruiter's eyes on your resume will also be a good way to make sure you know it looks good. They are the people who are expected to be career professionals. They will also be representing you through the process of interviewing. They should make it their goal to have as much pride in your background as you have.

Someone who is an expert also will be most likely the most connected. If they work specifically for an industry, it is much more likely they will have a connection to people within the industry. Working with these professionals will help you to get in touch with those you seek.

3. Coaching and tips

A good recruiter will only work with companies they understand well. It is the job of the recruiter to know the client they are working for, and how to meet their hiring needs. This often involves face-to-face meeting, a visit to the working office, and several follow-up calls. A steady stream of communication on their end will provide all of the updates on the company and the role to you, making you better equipped to present yourself the best way.

Before any interview, a recruiter should take the time to role-play with you. Make sure that they make the time to do so. It should be your priority to practice an interview before you arrive. This way, you can polish up on how you present your skills. The recruiter, being another expert in job searching, should be able to give you the tips to perfecting your answers and making them polished enough for the employer.

Plus, it will help shake off the nerves if you give it a test spin.

4. Updates

A recruiter should be your friend in the process of job hunting – on professional level. Just as they are receiving updates from their client, they should be communicated to you. Be sure you are open to receiving these updates. If your recruiter is spending a lot of time on you, it's up to you to return the favor and make time to chat with them. It shouldn't be seen as overbearing if they have you top of mind for open roles. You'll want to have your resume in front of as many opportunities as possible.

TIP: Make is very clear to a recruiter that you do not want them to submit your resume without first having your approval. This will prevent you wasting your times with companies in whom you are not interested. Being submitted to jobs you are not interested in also runs the risk of looking unprofessional in your industry.

It is also not a good look to cancel an interview or be a no-show. If you are not interested in a job, it is key to have that communicated before something is set up. Word tends to travel fast within industries. Looking bad to a company that you may come in contact with later in your career is a step in the wrong direction.

Should you work with several recruiters at a time?

The answer to this is within your power. The answer to this is generally *if you feel like it*. In theory, the more recruiters you have in your corner, the more opportunities you are bound to have put in front of you. The key is, however, keeping in mind what makes a good recruiter and what makes a bad recruiter.Making solid relationships with one recruiter is more advisable than working with several. Having a trustworthy, reliable recruiter will help you presently and in your future.

HOW TO FIND A RECRUITER

Going about finding a recruiter could be a search in itself. There are many recruiting agencies and staffing firms that specialize in different areas of expertise.

Start by doing a search for job agencies in your area. That will help narrow down where you should be sending your resume, and they will be able to pair you with someone on your team who can help. There are several free websites you can use to run the search for you and narrow down the options.

Sites like recommendedrecruiter.com, onlinerecruitersdirectory.com can be helpful in finding agencies in your area. Forbes also releases a list of the best firms in the nation - a good tool if your area is offered. It's also okay to reach out to some of the bigger firms even if they're not in your area. They could have some remote roles (if applicable) or some guiding points for you.

Keep in mind the several ways which agencies define them. Some common names you can search when conducting your search are: search agency, staffing agency, staffing firm, employment agency, or headhunter. There could be some others, but any of those common names will surely lead you in the right direction.

How to use LinkedIn contact recruiters

Use your network to find some of the decision makers who can help you get in touch with hiring managers or - better yet - the hiring managers themselves!

A good trick to applying online is to look at job boards and, instead of sending your resume through the ether with all the others, find the hiring manager on LinkedIn. Depending on how you are connected to them, you can send a message expressing your interest.

Example:

Hi Sheryl,

I hope his message finds you well. I saw your job posting on Monster and wanted to reach out directly to introduce myself. I think I'd be a great fit for the job and wanted to get in touch with you to discuss it more. Please don't hesitate to reach out.

Another helpful aspect of LinkedIn is that there is a built-in job board. You can apply directly to a job with your LinkedIn profile in lieu of your resume. The hiring manager or job-poster will receive your profile and can contact through the website. From there, you can send them a connection request showing that you are confident in having your profile reviewed further. Again, be sure to include a personalized message.

Hi Donna,

My profile should be on its way to you in regards to the Senior Analyst role, but I wanted to introduce myself to you personally. Please let me know if I can provide any additional content for my application. I look forward to connecting!

Even if there is not a job posted for a company, knowing their hiring team will help you stay top-of mind for when there is. These are good connections to have.

Hi Craig,

I hope you're doing well and on track to hit quota. I'd love to connect so we can network! I'm a Sales Specialist for my company and we had a booth near yours at last year's conference. I'll have to stop by and say hello next year. You all seem to have had some fun giveaways.

Congrats! Something on your profile or in your resume stood out. The first thing you'll need to do is find out what it is they are recruiting for. This can get a little tricky. A lot of recruiters will want your information first, so they can ensure whether or not it is worth the time to answer your questions and, down the line, submit you to a job.

Your time is valuable, too. There are important questions that you should be asking as well. It's going to be a give and take. Make sure to be respectful and don't leave the conversation hanging.

Make sure you find out what type of recruiting they do. Some agencies only recruit for temporary positions. If you are only looking for full-time, permanent roles, be open and honest about that. You'll also want to ask what their specialty is. Most recruiters and agencies have a specific industry for which they recruit. Don't waste your time barking up the wrong tree.

Recruiters do not have hiring power; they simply have connections. They work with a company to do all the legwork in finding candidates that may or may not be suitable for a role. After they find you, they present you to the company. The company then makes the decision if the candidate appears to be a good one. That means, they'll want to work with you to polish up the rough edges and ensure the client will approve. It's a win-win for all parties involved.

CHAPTER 4. GOING AT IT

ALONE

If you would like to weather the storm alone, there are ways you can go about doing this as well, but it starts the same way.

Make sure your resume and LinkedIn are up to date and match. It is an incredibly poor reflection on you if you appear to be unsure of your work history or trying to conceal something – both of which come off as the case to employers when these documents are unclear. This is the absolute first stage of any job search, with or without help of a staffing professional.

Once you have identified your personal industry, you have some research to do.

JOB BOARDS

Job Boards are often the first stop for job seekers. They provide a database to which you can include your resume and be discovered by employers. They also allow you to search for jobs that have been posted by the employers. Popular job boards include Monster.com, Indeed.com, CareerBuilder.com, SimplyHired.co, among others.

To navigate the job board, you will often be prompted to start by adding your resume. Adding your resume puts you in the database, which cans your resume for some key words. This will help as employers begin to create their searches and seek out professionals with the qualifications they seek. It is important to have your resume updated to reflect the industry for which you are applying.

The problem with these is that you only have access to jobs posted on the respective site, and most sites require the employer to have a paid membership to the platform.

It could also take quite some time to get discovered. The site is set up to have a revolving catalog of jobs posted. If a job exists that was not listed, you will not be able to find out about it through that particular site. Job boards are a good start for a passive job search.

Another limiting factor to job boards is that they do not often include the contact info for the employer, leaving you with the option only to wait and see if anything sticks.

If you are a passive job seeker, job boards can be a good option just to begin to weigh your options. To begin a full-throttle job search, LinkedIn is one of the best tools. With a database of millions of professionals, it provides a global Rolodex of people with hiring power. It takes more time to comb through, but following the right habits can help you zero in on what will be important to your career.

Start by researching your industry. Find out what some of the top companies in this industry are, and search them on LinkedIn.

As soon as you locate the company you are targeting, you will have the option of how you want to go about it. Always start by hitting "Follow" so you can stay on top of company news, updates, and job listings. Next to the Follow button is "See Jobs." That will take you to the LinkedIn job board, where you can search open positions and cater the results to your specific needs. LinkedIn will even have a few chosen that "match your skills."

From there you'll have the option to apply directly for the job.

TIP: You will also have the opportunity to make yourself stand out a little bit more. At the bottom of the job description should be scrolling box of people who work at the company. Scroll through and see if there are any connections you can make between the two of you. That will be a great way to reach out. It's okay to reach out and express your interest in the company. It could be the extra help you need getting through the door or provide a warm-welcome down the line. Keep making valuable connections on LinkedIn!

After you have applied for the job, you can also do a little research on their HR team (if it was not included in the "Who Works Here" section. Find them and send them a quick message or an email. Some hiring managers may have their email directly on their profile. Take that as a green light to reach out.

If not, an inMail will go a long way. Be sure always to make it personal!

ATTENDING NETWORKING EVENTS

We touched on networking via social media earlier in the book, but it is also important when you are going about job searching to get out there and pound the pavement. Networking events are a rare instance where everyone you want to talk to is in the same room.

Work the room! Go in and introduce yourself to someone, anyone!, and see where the conversation takes you. When you do get the chance to talk with someone, keep it semi-professional, semi-casual. Networking events are places for people to be around like-minded professionals. You can talk about work and the industry as a whole, but don't come with a resume and business cards forcing them into everyone's hand. Make yourself approachable and if you are approached, make yourself stand out!

It's okay to go with friends, but it does no help if you go with your friends, grab some free food and leave without meeting anyone. Although it may seem like you won something in the situation, you are losing a great opportunity to make connections for your future.

If you decide you are going to go with friends, go separately and have them meet you there. That could lead the way to them meeting someone before you get there, making the transition to more connections begin.

If you are both there, fan out in the room. You can teamwork to get to know some different people and, as social events go, meet back in the middle with some valuable connections.

The final, crucial piece of networking advice is to not overdo it. A networking event is kind of like a game: who can make the most connections while remaining the most sober. Make sure you are not too pushy with people, and that you aren't overstaying your welcome without being occupied by the task at hand.

CHAPTER 5. INTERVIEWING

So your recruiter got made time with the hiring manager or you were able to got put in front of a hiring manager by someone you met during networking. Congrats! Now you get the chance to make yourself shine brighter than your resume.

The interview is the moment when you get to show up and give it your all. (Well, not too much, remember you are trying to get a job.) What is being gauged here is how well you communicate, how well you are received, and whether or not you will fit in well with the company.

People have different ways of preparing for this experience, but the major key is to prepare. Do not leave it until the day of the interview to just "feel it out" or "go with the flow." The interviewer will undoubtedly be coming with a plan of attach on how to approach a possible employee. You will need to be your most alert as well.

HOW TO PREPARE:

Let's get this out of the way right away: a suit is no longer the universal standard for interviewing. More and more companies have opted to go the route of the business casual style. Wearing a full suit when it is not necessary could run you the risk of seeming out of touch. Make sure you know your potential-employer before making a decision. If all else fails, it is also okay just to ask.

DO work the question into a natural conversation when you are invited back for the interview

DON'T email the employer the night before asking for advice on what to wear.

Other ways to know what to wear are (yes, again) checking LinkedIn! Look at some of the profile pictures of the people who work there. If they are all professional-looking headshots with jackets and blazers on, it may be best to go with the business professional attire. If it is more relaxed buttoned shirts and blouses, business casual is probably acceptable.

Even if they are a lenient on wearing jeans, save it for when you have the job! Always tip more toward a more polished look than one that you think will fit in.

Key to office dress codes:

Business professional: Suits. Women may opt for a knee-length skirt and blazer. Men will normally dress in a suit.

Business casual: This is a bit more relaxed while remaining professional. Women should aim to wear shirts with sleeves and closed-toes shoes. Men can wear jeans so long as they wear a collared shirt.

Casual: There are more leniencies in casual environments that should be explored once you are hired and present enough to make the call. Stick to the business-type wear while you interview.

Ladies: a big question that always arises is whether or not you should wear heels to an interview. The answer is entirely up to you. If they make you feel empowering and are closed-toed, neat-looking shoes, feel free to wear them. If you they are you favorite pair of shoes that you are unable to walk in, opt for something shorter or flats. It should never be regarded as a poor decision to steer clear of heels. Be comfortable and you will exude confidence.

1. CREATE YOUR ELEVATOR PITCH

Your "elevator pitch" is your answer to the question "So, what do you do?" The idea is that, if you are in an elevator with someone, you have a very limited time to summarize and your experience, skills, and (hopefully) make a good impression. You want to be able to articulate who you are and what you do before they get the chance to get off at the next floor. Ideally, someone will be whipping out a business card! This pitch will be asked of you many times during interviewing as well. It is important to speak confidently and concisely about who you are as a professional.

How to construct your elevator pitch:

- What business are you in?

- How long have you been in this business/industry?

- Where did you come from/how did you get into the industry?

- What is your objective?

Here are a few examples of how to group those aspects together to really make you sparkle in under 30 seconds:

1. I have been working as a contract administrator for the last 3 years working, specializing in start-ups, helping employers to choose the right HR software

for their business and working with them for a smooth implementation before finding my next project.

2. I'm an intern at XYZ News Network working with the investigative team to complete a story to be released for Christmas time. I graduate in spring and hope to continue my career in the newsroom.

3. I'm a sales professional in the software industry for 2 years. I educate spas and salons in the Greater-Chicago area about our scheduling software, often attending trade shows nationwide to help connect with some national brands that may also be interested in using our product in the next year.

These answers are short, concise, and prove that you are a professional in your field doing something meaningful with plans to improve yourself in your role and the industry in which you work.

Study the role

When you go into an interview, you really have to know the job. The job description, in most cases, will be able to guide you through this. Make sure you study each one of the bullet points so that you know what is expected of you in this role.

TIP: the first few bullet points are generally the most important. Speak to those, and tie in your past experiences to present yourself as well equipped.

Most employers will not want to train someone new from the ground up to do a duty. They expect you to come into the role with the tools and knowledge to help you have a smooth transition into your new role. Granted, they will be teaching you the ways around the role in their company, and there will be a lot of learning as to how to communicate within the company. Every company is different. Don't show up as a know-it-all. You want to prove, also, that you're coachable.

DON'T ask about salary during the first, second, or even third conversation if the employer does not bring it up. It takes your motives away from the role. That should be saved for the negotiation phase and, most likely, they will know into what range your current salary falls.

Your Kryptonite

Before an interview, you are going to have to take a good look in the mirror. More likely than not, you will be asked about your weaknesses. Be prepared to answer it thoroughly and eloquently.

"This is a question to help measure a candidate's level of self-awareness," says hirer, Laura Attewell.

No employer wants to hear that you have no weaknesses; it is far from the truth. What that question is looking for is two things: to be honest without being cocky, and to

"A potential employer also wants to know how you plan to combat this weakness should you be signed on to the job," says Laura Attewell.

One way to answer this question is by identifying your strengths first. Recall moments from your job that really made you shine. Reflect on key accomplishments, major wins, quotas hit, clients signed, deadlines met, successful negotiations, et cetera, and identify then what might have suffered in order for you to get there. There will be a balancing act in all of it.

For instance, perhaps your last client signed was a tricky one, so you spent too much time on them and neglected your other clients.

Another instance of workplace weakness that can be resolved through some tweaking is burning out too quickly. People come in and work so ruthlessly in the first half of the day that the second half is spent wasted.

Sometimes, it can come down to something as simple as being too proud to ask for help in a situation.

You are not done when you find your weakness.

"If a weakness is stated, you must have an improvement plan already in mind to discuss," says industry professional Laura Attewell.

Create your game plan. This can be anything from buying a planner to write in your appointments or putting your email alerts on to making sure you leave the office on time. Maybe it is making sure you take periodic breaks to stretch your legs or drink some water so you can stay fresh throughout the day. Whatever will counteract your weakness is a good answer!

There are many ways to balance out your weaknesses once you identify yours. Make sure it is something that pertains to the job.

THE RIGHT ANSWERS

Though there is no definitive "right" answer to interview questions, there are specific tracks you can go down in order to be someone who stands out.

Aside from the question of understanding your weaknesses, there will be many other questions during an interview that will be very telling to the interview. Some major companies have become notorious for dishing out questions that seem to be coming from left field.

They are not. These questions are designed to see how you think, how quickly you think, and how well you can relay an answer.

Take SpaceX; according to career resource site GlassDoor, it has been reported that the company has been known to ask, "When a hot dog expands, in which direction does it split and why?" For the science behemoth, this question is an attempt to understand the depth of one's knowledge. It's a fairly simple scientific happening (considering the employer is famously working on how to sustain life on Mars), but the question should be answered in a way that exhibits the candidate's knowledge.

In a different concept of curiosity, an employer may also want to know to know what makes you tick. Knowing some things about a candidate and what type of person they are is good insight for choosing the next person to work at a company.

Software platform HubSpot asks new employees: "If you had $40,000 to start a business, what would you start?"

This answer is looking for a few different things. It may be hoping to hear something very insightful or inventive come up. This shows the employer that you are creative and have a very productive vision.

It could also be answered in a way that reveals your true passions. Our passions oftentimes correlate to some of our strengths. It is good for an employer to get a sense of what drives you in order for you to be successful.

DON'T ramble on! A good answer is concise, full of useful information, and last about 30 seconds.

It is a good idea to get your brain bending to the idea of being hit with some strange questions. Here is a collection of a few questions that could be asked and how to answer them.

"How many basketballs would fit in this room?"

This question is meant to see how quickly you can (ahem) bounce back. Initially, it seems daunting. Surely in the context of an interview you are not expecting to have to fill a room with basketballs. However alarming, keep your cool.

This question is referencing one variable that is universally known: the size of a basketball. On face value, you may be lead to believe that it is asking the question for an absolute answer, much like the game of counting candy in a jar. The interview is not looking for a specific answer – they are looking for how you answer this question.

A key to answering this question is to do it in your own fashion. Roll with the though process you are having. Do not clam up and go silent, actually trying to measure the length and width. Instead, ask some important rebuttal questions: Are they inflated or deflated? Is that assuming the furniture will remain in the room or be taken out? Asking these questions proves to the interviewer that you can be given a task and are willing to do the work to complete it.

"How many windows are there in New York City?"

This question is similar to the one about the basketballs. It is trying to figure out how you go about analyzing information. If you throw out a number without thinking, it will look like you are hasty, panicked, and not thorough. What you want to do is work through how you would, if given more information, figure this out.

Since NYC runs on a grid, you can audibly start to summarize the number of streets there are with an approximation of how many are on each block .

Another way you can do this is by referring to population density. How many people live in NYC? How many of them are likely to have at least one window in their home? In their office?

No matter how your brain starts to try to process this information, present it as you are willing to work to figure it out.

"What flavor ice cream would you be?"

A little less analytical; a little more fun; a little less likely. If a company is asking a personalized question as such, they want to hear some personality come out of it. There are a lot of flavors of ice cream thanks to Ben and Jerry's, so if you choose an exotic flavor, be sure to have reason.

Say you choose rocky road – you can say that you like to go about life in a way that you have some cushion between some of the difficult situations is life. You take time for yourself.

If you want to say vanilla, then own vanilla! Let your employer know what makes you the universally recognizable flavor without making you sound bland.

FEELING OUT YOUR INTERVIEWER

When you go into an interview, remember this: the interviewer is the one with something to provide to you. Though you are interviewing for a role in which you will be providing services to a company through the completion of your duties, you are hoping to appease the company so that they want to have you sign on. Allow yourself to be open to the interviewer.

A big part of what they are measuring in a meeting is how you will fit with the team. Are you someone who talks over someone else? Try to keep that in check. You are there just as much to sell yourself to the employer as you are to get information on the role. Make the time worth everyone's while and be respectful.

Keep in mind that you want to sell them only the most relevant parts of your profile. If there is a connection between the two of you, use it your advantage and learn more about the lifestyle of the role.

Allow them to set the pace for the interview. Nothing is worse than picking up the wrong vibes from someone and completely clashing. Make sure that you go in and match their tone and energy.

Above all, have respect. Understand that they are taking time from their day to meet with you. Be appreciative and respectful in that you make it worthwhile.

FOLLOWING UP

Before you leave an interview, you should always have the interviewer's contact details. Most of the time they will have set up the time to speak with you, so you already have it. If there were several different employees with whom you met, be sure to ask your initial interviewer their contact details before you leave, or ask them for a business card when you meet, if they do not give it to you immediately.

You will want to be able to send them a thank you note.

A thank you not is paramount in your interviewing process. **Every single employer, no matter what your industry is, will want to see that you took the time to follow up and thank him or her for his or her time.** A lot of times, when it is between two or more candidates, they will opt for the one who took the time to send the note. Make your profile stand out and be the person that sends it.

Your thank you note should be brief, but personalized. Thank the person for their time, express your furthered interest in the role.

DON'T expect a thank you letter to be responded to. It is a key for them to receive, but you will get your response when they all have time to discuss if you are a good fit for the company.

Example:

Hi Leslie,

Thank you for taking the time to meet with me this afternoon. It was so wonderful to meet you and hear more about how we could work together on the creative team. It was so interesting to learn some of the lengths you go for marketing inspiration! I could see myself flourishing in such an open-minded environment.

Hope to hear from your team soon!

Once the interview is over, your thank you note should be sent before the day is over; next morning at the absolute latest. You want them to have a full picture of you as a candidate before they make the decision. The time you took to send a thank you note will go a long way.

You should hear back about the interview within three days. Often times it is not only you in the running for a job. Interviewing is also not the only job function that the hiring manager has during their day. Respect that they have other duties to tend to. If you do not hear back within a week, you can send a gentle email just so you stay on their radar and can reiterate your interest.

Example:

Hi Leslie!

I hope your week is going well. I wanted to touch base after meeting last week. Please let me know what next steps might be or if you'll need anything addition from me.

If they ask you to come back for another interview, wonderful! Now is the time to stay sharp. Most of the time, they will have you meet with other members of the team.

TIPS:

-Don't be robotic. They're going to want to meet you after talking to teammates who have already met you. You're going to have to tell your story (aka- your elevator pitch) several times over. Always make sure it's as if it's the first time.

-Do your research! Find some more members of the team and be able to ask questions about their role

In some roles, the final interview takes place as a mock-sale or presentation. Practice your presentation before you are set to deliver it. If your recruiter has the time, make an effort to meet and have him or her be your audience. Delivering your presentation well is going to be your last chance at making an impression. Keep in mind all of the public speaking tips such as projecting your voice and making eye contact.

Sealing the deal

Once you arrive at the grueling end of interviewing, you will probably need a nap or a drink. However, you should never assume you have a new job until the ink is dry! Most of the time there will be a verbal agreement, but don't quit your job until you see the contract. You still have time to decide if it is the right choice for you.

Be sure you know what is expected of you when you are offered a job. Get all of the information you need before you begin celebrating. Find out about compensation, position, benefits, and start date. Normally, there will be an oral offer issued before a formal written contract. Try to get all of the information you need orally, so that you know what to expect. It will be best not to have to go back and forth in renegotiating a contract once it is already drawn up.

Chapter 6. Changing Careers

We have talked a lot about building off of your foundation to grow your career through job changes, but sometimes you want to leave the field you're in completely. Career changes are possible, but a completely different prey to wrangle. There is a lot to learn, and a lot to leave behind, when you begin anew in a different industry. Before you make the decision to switch careers, ask yourself some very important questions pertaining to WHY?

Why You Should Change Careers?

1. You didn't choose the field; the field chose you

Oftentimes, people graduate college and feel desperate, or even excited, to land a job. Taking the first job that sticks is often a very impactful learning experience. Sometimes, it opens your eyes to challenges and passions you were unaware to have had. Sometimes, you can fake your love of the work for long enough to sustain a paycheck.

At some point, when the music cuts off, a decision needs to be made. Will you see yourself continuing to climb in this field? Is there a burnout already on the horizon? Do you feel as though you are not being challenged enough anymore? These are just a few signs that your job may not be a good one for you.

Be sure that you make a very thoughtful decision when you find yourself having these thoughts. Sometimes, it is not the role but the company that is not the best fit for you. Other times, you are just in need of a new challenge, or a different team. There are many variables that relate to how you can feel more fulfilled.

When the answer seems unclear, you have to go to a very base-level understanding of your role. What are your daily duties? Which of those duties do you enjoy? If there are many of them, then it is most likely not the job that is giving you a sense that you want to leave.

If you find that much of what your job entails is making you unhappy, it can be time for a switch.

Perhaps you are in sales, and you are still struggling with cold calling. That would lead you to understanding what else you can do at your job. Perhaps it is making meaningful connections with people through various other networking options. If the idea of that also sounds cumbersome to you without providing any opportunity for happiness, it may not be the right job for you.

Get to the depths of what is making you unhappy. If you find that your desk and everything surrounding it is the cause, it could be time to relocate.

2. New technology is making your role obsolete

There was a point in time when people used to read through catalogs of goods and place orders over the phone. There would be representatives on the other end, taking the order and having it shipped. As the technological big bang, also known as the Internet, became accessible, order clerk jobs dwindled.

You may not see your job dwindling until it is too late. As technology continues to automate more processes, more and more jobs are becoming obsolete. The good thing is, there are also many other industries emerging ripe with opportunity.

Technology is continuously morphing in ways that make it more engrained in our society. There are many different options for jobs within technology, including sales, implementation, engineering, and coding.

A recent surge in a need for software coding has had people taking a shot at the computer programming skills via various courses. This would have been reserved for the "computer nerds" in days of yore, but in this age, everyone is a computer nerd. We are all interconnected through the web and via or devices.

3. You are interested in an emerging technology

As technology becomes more and more prominent, coding has thrown itself into one of the top career-choices in the world. Currently there are about 3.6 million coders in the US, and about 18.2 million worldwide. Evans Data Corp expects a 46% increase in that number by 2019. That's a lot of opportunity.

What is important to remember is that working in programming or software is not a quick remedy to your career woes. It takes a lot of practice, effort, and training to be good at it and successful, but like any career, that takes an investment of time. According to the expected boom of jobs in that field, it could be a good investment for someone looking to switch up their career.

There are, however, other opportunities in technology, as listed above. The typical office job may now incorporate much more technology than before, like human resources software or scheduling software. Any job can be updated. If you are feeling like you are missing all of the new technology, maybe it is time to stretch your legs in the field and see where you can fit.

4. You want to use your passion for work

Perhaps you have not given into the hype of electronics and technology. There are still incredible amounts of jobs that need to be done the good old-fashioned way. Picking up a trade is a great option for people looking to switch careers. There are many Trade Schools that offer part-time programs, allowing you to make money and still go to school. There are also full-time programs that can get people certified and ready to work within months. It all depends on what type of trade speaks to you.

Electricians, hairdressers, builders, and many other professional options exist for people who no longer necessarily want to report to a traditional office. Think about some hobbies you have in your spare time, or topics that interest you that you find yourself spending time researching and learning. These side-projects could turn into a full-time, full-blown career.

Sometimes, a career-change can be a slow realization over time. Sometimes, it could come in one deciding tidal wave. Either way, it is important to know when the right time is for you to think about making the switch.

II. Stepping into the role you want

If you fall into any of those five categories, changing careers is a good option for you. If you find that your role is what is making you unhappy, it could also be a chance to talk with some of your managers about switching up your responsibilities. There are a few different ways in which you can go about making a switch, from internal sliding to a complete revamp of your skillset.

1. Changing your role within your company

Depending on your position within the company and the company structure, there could be opportunity to take on a different role that fits better with what you envision yourself doing. To do this, you must come incredibly prepared with your angle. Talk to your manager or supervisor and discuss some of your accomplishments and skillsets. Decide where you would like to use them more, and present yourself as a valued member of the team. Come prepared with how you will make an impact in a new role and why you are an ideal candidate to take on a new challenge. You have a lot of power in this position if you have done well in your current role.

Beware! You do not want to come off as unhappy in your role, or they might begin to take steps to replace you out completely. Your angle should represent your desire to grow and continue to contribute to the vision of the brand.

2. Work for a company you believe in, let the role follow

Perhaps you are an industry-changer, or you are looking for a new company with a different product or mission; you have the opportunity to leave your job and market your skills to different roles. It can be a productive transition to use what you have already accomplished much in your role.

At times, new employers will want to see that you have been accomplished in a role; this will necessitate a lateral move. Don't be fearful of taking them if it is an investment for your career path. If there is a company you believe in more than another, make it your goal to join them. The passion and the drive will be easier to exhibit, giving you an opportunity to be seen as someone who can take on new and different challenges.

Be sure to be honest about your intentions in the interview. It is a perfectly valid reason for wanting to move into a new company.

Your reason could sound something like this:

I am attracted to the product of this company and believe I can be a valuable asset to the sales team. My most recent skills are all sales-focused but I hope in the future to be able to use them and be able to work with the marketing team.

You can sound eager for a job even if it is not your envisioned end goal as long as you are honest about what is!

3. Clean slate

Starting a new is the most challenging method for job seekers, but it is the least limiting. However difficult, it is doable. Here is the most important time for tying in transferable skills, which will be gone over in depth in Chapter 7.

It is also incredibly important when you are changing careers to work your network. Before you take a leap for the side in which the grass looks greener, ask! Reach out to some people who are in that industry. Are they people you can envision yourself working with?

Ask about the role. You want to try to get a feel for the industry you are about to enter. Starting over is fine. Starting over again and again can get tiring. Try to make the most educated decisions possible.

Ask questions such as:

How much teamwork do you incorporate into your work?

Do you often have to put in long hours?

What were the biggest obstacles in achieving your goals at work?

How much time do people usually spend in the role?

Is there a lot of turnover?

There is no right time or wrong time to change career - it comes from your own personal decisions. What you need to consider is if you have enough of the drive to be able to take on a new challenge. There will inevitably be a learning curve, no matter how many transferrable skills you have already. Be open to change and coaching.

MARKETING YOURSELF TO NEW EMPLOYER - HARNESSING TRANSFERRABLE SKILLS

Whether you are just starting out looking for a career or you are looking to change your career, harnessing your transferrable skills will be a huge bolster for your resume. There are many aspects of you as a human that can make you a good option for an employee.

Some skills you may consider yourself to have (but not limited to):

- Adaptability

Being able to learn the layout of your new environment and successfully transition into it is an incredible skill to have, especially when you are seeking employment. Hirers do not want people who are stuck in their own ways and unwilling to learn a new landscape.

Someone who is adaptable will know how to take the things they learned in one place and still have an open-mind to learn how things work in another. If you are to claim adaptability, ensure that you have some way to illustrate. Maybe you moved from a big, brand name company into a small business. Be open to recounting your experience and providing details as to how you made the transition.

- Communication

It may seem like everyone can communicate, but it really is a rare and incredibly important skill to have.

Imagine you are in a role on a team of five. If three of your members work together on part of a project without informing the others on the team, they run the risk of not having synchronization through their work. Someone may have wasted their time doing what has already been done, or they have taken the project in a wrong direction

Communication also goes the other way. Listening is a massive part of this category considering you are charged with giving and taking information in a communicative exchange. Habits of good communication come when you do well with what you are told to do and can report back with the updates.

If you are one of the people who like to know what updates on what everyone else on your team is doing, you may consider describing yourself as having good communication skills.

- Coachability

Coachability is the new adaptability (kind of). It differs in that when you define yourself as "coachable," you are expressing your good ability to work with being given instruction. Many people who are coachable are those that take others' advice and implement it into their job to produce better work.

- Conflict resolution

An incredibly useful tool in professional and personal life, conflict resolution is a value asset to market to employers. Perhaps there was a hiccup in service at the restaurant you previously worked at. Finding the grace to be able to come to a mutual point that everyone is again satisfied is a value skill. It required a calm and collected nature with an end-goal in mind.

This is a trait that should certainly be backed by example if you are going to cite it as a skill.

- Hard Working

Many people claim to be hard working; few truly are. This is best exhibited in how you can back it up. Perhaps you had to go back to school while keeping a part-time job. That is indeed perceived as a hard-working trait (as well as organized). Perhaps you had a project due that one of your partners opted out of or dropped the ball on. There are many personal situations where you can depict yourself as hard working.

Be cautious if you use this to explain yourself and you fall a bit on the lazy side. It will be noted and just because you sounded good in the interview does not mean it can save you during your time as an employee.

- Leadership

Being a part of a team can also give you the opportunity to be a leader. Being a leader has a very specific set of credentials. If you ever held a role in which you were in charge of the decision-making, you have been a leader. That can be in a job as a project manager, in a club as a president, or even a blogger who created their own site. To claim to be a leader, you are also very communicative and hard working, another two intangible qualities that will show with time.

- Motivation

There is a driving force behind everything. Understanding some of yours will help to land you in the category of a motivated worker. The value of motivation is that it is something that spreads. It is something that a person on a team can transmit to their fellow colleagues, making it a valuable aspect.

- Teamwork

When you are looking to get hired, you are looking to become the new kid on the block. Your employer wants to know that you will get along nicely with those who are already there. Adaptability helps in this aspect, but teamwork really makes it shine. Teamwork means you are not afraid to ask for help in a situation in which it is mutually beneficial. In a new job, you want to be as open as possible to learning methods of other people's work and ensuring that you can get the job done together.

- Time-management

For many just starting out in any industry, employers often want to know that you have the discipline to meet deadlines and work in a timely fashion. They also want to ensure that you will be on time and in attendance at meetings or scheduled events.

Perfect attendance can be a way to illustrate your ability to hold yourself accountable. You can also illustrate this trait by detailing your ability to juggle several projects under time restraints.

These intangibles are *soft skills* that will help you present yourself as a good candidate. Your *hard skills* are the things that are listed in your resume as the things you are equipped to and experienced in doing.

CHAPTER 7. PLANNING A

GRACEFUL EXIT

Your resignation

Finding a new job is exciting, although sometimes bittersweet. It comes with the inevitability of having to resign. Planning your exit from an employer may seem to be a messy situation. It is a breakup – someone is undoubtedly hurt in the process. There are still ways to go about it so that you are left with a bridge still standing.

Before you gear up for the conversation, make sure you have all of your ducks in a row with your new employer. There are a few very important things that must be dealt with to solidify your position:

1. Offer letter

Did you get your offer letter from your new employer? Do not make the mistake of relying only on a verbal offer. Make sure that there is a contract in place that thoroughly states the job is ready for you.

Also take a look at the contract to be sure that it is what you expected. This is where salary and bonuses is okay to talk about. You will want to make sure that there is no communication on this or any other aspect of the role to which you are signing.

Aside from salary are benefits. Find out how you will be able to enroll under the company's new plan. Your new employer should want to be as honest and upfront about the process as possible. Hold them accountable to do so.

2. Start Date

After all parties necessary sign the offer letter, make sure you have a time and place to arrive to when the smoke clears. Stranger things than a contract falling through have happened. Don't jump ship without a life vest.

If you are all set to begin your new job, it is time to tell your employer.

In most situations, it is customary to give your employer two weeks' notice of your departure. This time period is meant to allow you to tie up your loose ends and for the employer to get the chance to fill the role.

Be conscious that, in some situations, the two-week time period may be skipped all together and you could be "walked-out," or asked to clear your desk and escorted out immediately. This happens if there is sensitive information that you had worked on, thus denying the opportunity to remove it from the premises within the coming weeks. If the new company to where you are going is a competitor, this is a very common practice.

Assuming that you are going to have the opportunity to stay on and slowly hand off your duties to colleagues, there are a few things to keep in mind before you have the conversation about leaving.

1. Have a plan for how you are going to hand-off your responsibilities. You do not want to leave a mess

in your departure – that will only tarnish your reputation with your employer. Make sure you are aware of your duties and what you need to tie up is closed, and what you need to transfer to a colleague is ready to be transferred.

2.Do not let the cat out of the bag too soon. It will reflect poorly on you if you have word floating around the office that you are planning to leave before you get the chance to tell those to whom you report. Allow for them to have the respect of receiving this information directly from you.

Once you are ready to provide them the reason behind your departure, make sure you thought about it fully. How will you gracefully explain to them your reason for leaving? Make sure this is premeditated. You may have some qualms that had inspired you to begin looking for work opportunities. Do not go into the conversation angrily. Instead, think of it as a sad farewell and a thank you for their faith in you as an employee.

Scheduling a meeting to share the news

When possible, schedule some time to talk with your manager or supervisor to let them know in person your intention to leave the company. Before anyone else, you should let your manager or direct supervisor know first. It is a very professional approach, and respectful of their position. It is important to keep things that way by remaining positive, or, at the least, neutral, in the process. Don't burn your bridge too soon.

This meeting will ideally be with the person who oversees you, or hired you. Be prepared for this interaction by doing some reflecting on the job. Let them know some areas in which you felt you were happy, stimulated, challenged, or supported. It will go a long way in being appreciative of the partnership.

Make sure you thank them for the opportunity Whether or not you loved or hated the job, it is a very important thing that you express gratitude for being given it. Do not forget all the work you put in to get the shot there in the first place! This will also lend itself to the professionalism of carrying on in good standing.

You will also want to explain your position. The will expect some sort of explanation as to why you are leaving. Keep in mind not to say anything poorly about them, but be honest.

Some things to consider as your reason for leaving are:

- Career growth

- Commute time

- Dream job offer

- Great opportunity

- More/less travel

- Better pay

- Restructuring of the company

Be careful to cite money as your only motivation to leave. Though sometimes it may come into play (i.e.- if you are an expectant mother or have very specific needs to meet that are becoming difficult), it is not the strongest nor most respectable way to leave a job. It often just shows that your time spent there was only valued monetarily instead of as an important step in your career. If better pay is the main reason, frame it in the sense that you are more interested in a different company culture that fits your life at the present time.

RESIGNATION LETTER

Before your meeting with you boss, have your resignation letter ready. This can be the last note written to your employer, thanking them for your time spent there. They may ask you to write this after your meeting, so come prepared. Keep it brief, polite, and specific. Unless otherwise discussed or anticipated, include the date that is set to be your last.

If you did not have a chance for a meeting, your resignation letter will have to include some of the information that would have been expected in person.

A good resignation letter will include positive feedback of the employer and a specific date, presumably two weeks away, when you will end your duties with them.

It is also recommended to leave your contact information. This way, co-workers will be able to stay in touch and network further down the line. Don't burn any bridges!

Example:

Dear Jane,

It is with the unfortunate news I am writing you today to let you know I have decided to take a job offer. My last day here will be [two weeks from date of the letter]. I will be glad to stay to complete any unfinished duties and ensure that the transition is smooth as possible for my coworkers.

It has been a very rewarding time working for [Company name] and I wish you nothing but the best in all future endeavors.

Please know that I would be very happy to keep in touch.

Again, this is a common way to leave a job, but opt for the meeting if you have the chance, or if you have a rapport with your boss and want to be met with mutual respect.

Exit Interview

There is the possibility of an exit interview. These should be a positive experience in order for you to let the employer know how you have grown in the role and feedback as to what you experienced and what they should be able to mold from that going forward.

Do your best to keep the information you share positive! A good tactic for doing this is by venting beforehand. Yes, venting. There are naturally frustrations within your job. Make sure you do not end up getting into a tussle in the meeting room for letting out your anger on the last day. Vent beforehand to someone you trust, and work out what comes down to your feelings and what comes down to how the job can and should be done in the future. Though you may be frustrated with something or someone at work, your exit interview is not meant to air that out.

Some common questions you may be asked during an exit interview:

- *Why are you leaving?*

This will be asked if nothing else is, in one form or another. If you are leaving a job, the employer understands that something must have not been right for you. Be honest. Just try to be positive.

- *Did you feel well equipped to do your job?*

If you are leaving for another employer for a similar role, it will almost definitely be asked about how you felt you were able to conduct your work there. They will want to know how they can make their company a more enticing one to work for by being on top of what the in-demand practices and technology is.

- *How was your relationship to your manager?*

Though it may sound like they are jumping from one thing to another fairly quickly, it is important for HR to know how their employees work with those whom are in charge. It is important for managers to be helpful and present. Provide true, but positive feedback amidst your critique.

I.e. - *"Jerry was very devoted to the clients and in doing so he often signed us up to complete more projects than we could handle at once. It's very ambitious, but I hoped for some more communication with the team."*

Unless there are incredibly extenuation circumstances as to why you have decided to leave, you should always do your best to leave on a good note. These employers are now part of your network. They may be contacted in regards to your performance, you will want them to have positive things to say.

DON'T update your LinkedIn profile to reflect your new job until, at the earliest, you start your first day. You don't want to be too eager. Really, anything can happen. You'll also want the green light from your new job to be representing their brand. Many times, there are specific ways in which they like to uphold their online presence. Be respectful of everyone involved and be patient with the process.

COMBATTING THE COUNTEROFFER

Assuming you had been a valuable and productive employee, it may be hard for your company to watch you go. Many times, they will come back to you with a counteroffer. It is widely discouraged to accept them. Though it may provide you some of the things you had hoped for in your new job in a comfortable, familiar environment, it could change how you are perceived at work. Telling your employer you that you want to leave, unhappy or otherwise, and then deciding to stay can reflect poorly on you going forward.

In the most blunt of terms in the harshest of situations, if they offer to keep you it is only until they find a worthy replacement, leaving you back at square one.

Going through the job-hunting process is time-consuming. Once you arrive at a decision, stick to it. Stay firm in your decision and politely decline, offering your support of the company and the willingness to continue to be part of their network.

CHAPTER 8. TECH TALK

We talked a lot about buzzwords through the book, so now it is time to take a closer look at what some of them are, what they mean, and why they are important.

Though there are many industries with their own lingo and language, the technology industry in Silicon Valley and around the globe is booming so heavily that there are a lot of things to know within it. We will start there.

The beauty of learning the tech industry is that it (*ahem*) virtually translates into any and all industries. As the tech industry booms, it impacts (or disrupts, which we will get to in just a moment) all of the other industries that benefit from it. That could include any and all creative fields. It could also reach into business and finance field. It all depends how cutting-edge a company is.

It is important to ensure that you yourself are in the know in the latest developments. Here is a curated list of buzzwords used within and without the tech industry that you will want to say you know when you hear them.

A CRASH-COURSE TO THE LANGUAGE OF EMERGING TECHNOLOGY

(Alphabetically)

A/B testing

Often used in marketing and analytics, this is the process of trying two separate versions of something and seeing which one works better. In essence, it is a controlled experiment with two variants.

Application Programming Interface (API)

Called API amongst tech professionals, in extremely layman's terms, this is the code that was already written to and makes writing more code easy. It is the socket that exists already that allows the plug to be inserted and work.

The value of API is that the code writing does not have to be done every time a new technology is introduced. It is the groundwork and framework for allowing one program to speak to another, regardless of its home base.

Picture it as a loading screen. The time it takes for you to get from one page to another is the API working to translate one website to another.

Back-end

Commonly used when referring to "back-end development" or "server side," this is everything that happens behind the scenes or out of the eye of the customer. It is all of the coding that is done to create the presentation of a finished software or website. (See also: front-end)

Big data

All of the information that is too vast and complex to be understood or decoded by traditional data processing software. This comes into play when there is software that is specifically known as "big data software." This is NASA-level information that needs a place to be easily stored and revisited. Big data software helps to break it all down and present it.

Bounce or Bounce rate

When a website is visited too briefly, it's called "bounce." Bounce refers to how often someone visits the site and leaves before they get the information they were hoping for or purchase what's been offered. It is a term that is important amongst sales and design teams. Decreasing bounce means you are doing something that is attracting customers to your site and having them stay for enough time that you benefit from the visit.

The Cloud

Also used when discussing "cloud computing;" the method in which none of your data is stored on the hardware of the computer, but all in the intangible cloud. The cloud, put very simply, is the Internet. It is the where things are stored, cataloged, and accessible without it taking up precious memory on a hard-drive.

Conversion

Often used to gauge success in online marketing, conversion measures the success of a click on an ad turning into a purchase against a click on an ad that does not. This is the successful counterpart of bounce rate.

Crowd-funding

In a world of startups, there is a lot of talk about "crowd-funding." This is what they call the money they collect from several different investors or contributions that go into starting a business.

Data mining

When you have astronomical amounts of data to work with or learn from, data mining is how you can digest, decipher, and find patterns in the data that will be useful. It does the computing of the data to find patterns and predict future outcomes of the data provided.

Disruptive

Everyone wants to be disruptive in the age of technology. This is the term used to define a company whose technology has made another practice obsolete. Think of it literally as big powerful force that interrupts a task. It does not destroy though, and that is the major difference. Disruptive technology helps to improve the landscape by making processes more manageable.

Engagement

Any interaction someone has with a post creates an engagement. This could be a retweet, a Facebook 'like,' or a LinkedIn comment; basically it is anything that opens up a two-way interaction. Engagement comes into play a lot in marketing and advertising departments. It is a term that is used to refer to how many times people have clicked on something that has been put in front of them (usually strategically).

Front-end

The opposite of back-end, this refers to what becomes the user experience. The coding, or HTML, CSS, and JavaScript, work to translate the information to the proper screen to create a formatted user-experience.

Growth-hacking

Methods in which a specific person or party experiments to find new avenues to push a product. This is often external of the marketing team, as this person is skilled in understanding the landscape of the product and exactly how to expand it further.

HTML (HYPERTEXT MARKUP LANGUAGE)

Simply put, the language used to create web pages and applications.

Impressions

As opposed to engagement, where a viewer or user clicks on an ad or makes a mark on it, and impression something that simply is seen. Marketers use this term a lot to gauge how often they have appeared in front of a potential client without it being measured as translation into sales or success rate.

Internet of Things

Literally, what is around us; the Internet of things can sometimes be mistaken for the Internet that is full of possibilities. The Internet of things refers to all of our devices that have Internet connectivity and how they connect with one another.

Marketing Automation

There are many different ways to automate marketing, but as a conglomerate it is the use of different tools that place your ads in the most ideal spots through algorithms. It will find who is the most likely to be impacted (or to make an impression on) by the placement of the ad in their browser. It helps to scan the Internet and understand demographics of who is active online.

Wearables or Biowearables

See also: Internet of things. Wearables are things like our Smart Watches or modern step-counters that are able-to-be-worn and access the Internet, receiving and feeding data.

User-Generated Content (UGC)

This is Internet lingo for "word on the street." UGC is a collection of information from consumers, not paid advertising content, that is made public. It can often be reviews left on a product or a restaurant.

User Interface

The computer's ability to translate data to a user is part of the user interface. It is the graphic design, so to speak, of a piece of computer information. It defers from designing in that there is a technical aspect to this process. (See also: UX)

User Experience

Often working professionally together, UX comes into place when creating a way to engage within the webpage. It makes the UI look and feel possible by making sure it is functional.

(See also: UI)

Virtual Reality or VR

Products that have the ability to manipulate the senses to reflect what is on a screen. It is the opportunity to be immersed into something that is not real.

Software as a service (SaaS)

SaaS refers to all of the software that is available for hire by a company to provide a service to the client. There are many types of software that can be sold as a service, but the main component is that it is almost always subscription-based and hosted in a database (or the cloud).

Search Engine Optimization(SEO)

The process in which a person or organization methodically includes words or phrases that will make them more likely to appear in a search naturally (or organically) rather than having a paid-for ad.

CHAPTER 9. CREATING YOUR 5-

YEAR PLAN

No matter what you have chosen to do at this point, keep in mind where you hope to be in five years. An employer may ask you the same question, and it will be a little bit more of a jarring experience. They are hoping to see that you have thought about it and that you are taking thoughtful steps at achieving what you have set out to do.

This is another interview question that you should consider when practicing for an interview, but it is also something that you should workshop in your free time. It will help you understand how to manage juggling between your personal life and your career path - a crossroads that is exceedingly difficult to level out.

HOW TO BEGIN CREATING YOUR 5-YEAR PLAN

1. Where have you been?

In starting to create your plan, figure out what you did to get where you are. Reflect on the interview processes and try to recall where you were really impressive and where you fell flat.

Example: Perhaps you worked in a newsroom in college, and then became a production assistant when you began your career. Which aspects of that were more appealing to you?

Create a list of the things that stand out to you as accomplishments throughout your career. Were they meaningful to you? Did they lead to another place where you found a sense of fulfillment? These could be great indicators of what to continue to work toward, and what to leave behind.

What I achieved	How did it make me feel?

Understanding your accomplishments and how the made you feel will be an excellent tool in finding out where you want to go next.

Take a moment to use the above chart and fill out the top 3 things you feel you have accomplished. When you are done, rate them, 1 being the most fulfilling, 3 being the least.

2. Where do you hope to go?

After you have uncovered some of the things that have resonated with you, start to think about the possible places it can take you. If you have a clear vision of a project that you think you can handle, write it in a box with some notes on how you can get there.

When you get a clear idea of what your ambitions are, rate those as well. Which ones are in your power to complete right now? Which will take some time to organize? These things will help you to uncover where you might be within the next 1-2 years of your career.

What I want to	The tools I can use to get

accomplish	there

3. What are you strengths?

In looking at what you have achieved, it is important to start to identify how you got there. If you have already uncovered the answer to "What are your weaknesses?" back in Chapter 2, then your strengths should not be far behind.

Knowing your strengths will be helpful in uncovering what your next step should be in your career. When you are looking to the future, you can take the time to concentrate on what makes you continue to find success.

After you do understand your strengths, it will aid you in understanding better how you can use your identified tools to get you to the next step you want to be.

I want to accomplish: moving to California within the next two years and working as a project manager.	Tools I can use to get there: working my network that I have built and using my ability to connect with people for more information on open roles and leads on new jobs.

Once you understand the tools you have, you can better understand how well you can or will have to learn to use them.

4. What do you value most? What drives you?

Of what is uncovered at this point, you should be able to clearly see what your strengths you have. Some innate desire to succeed, as well as your own personal driving forces, is the pivotal foundations of these strengths. Take a look at the tables you have completed above. Ask yourself what you needed to do in order to achieve those goals. Also, ask yourself how you are going to maintain the tools in your arsenal to achieve your next set of goals.

In creating a plan for your future you will often find that some things do not fit. Try to uncover some things in your personal or professional life that have inhibited you from getting where you want to go.

In the other hand, look for things that have been a catalyst for you in your decision-making so far. Perhaps you first chose one job over another because they had free lunch. That means, you value a work environment that has a nurturing and attentive sense to it. Does this follow suit in your personal life?

Find out what makes you tick; get rid of what grinds your gears to a stop.

5. Finding a balance between these things, how will you be where you should be?

Do not forget to keep track of what happens in your personal life and how it helps you achieve your goals at work. Make it your mission to work to live, not to live to work. As the old adage goes: "love what you do and you'll never work a day in your life."

Perhaps going into any job will still feel like work for you - but it is where you can find fulfillment in and outside of work that makes it worthwhile, and can be the shaping of a career.

CONCLUSION

The expectation is that if you have reached this point in the book, you are ready to go out and find your dream job and career fulfillment! It is a long road, and this has been a long journey. The wonder is that if you ever find yourself tripping over the process again, you can revisit these pages and find inspiration and insight again. You are not expected to remember it all, but you are expected to take something from these pages and turn it into what you want out of work.

You have what you need, now go get what you want!

Made in the USA
Middletown, DE
27 January 2018